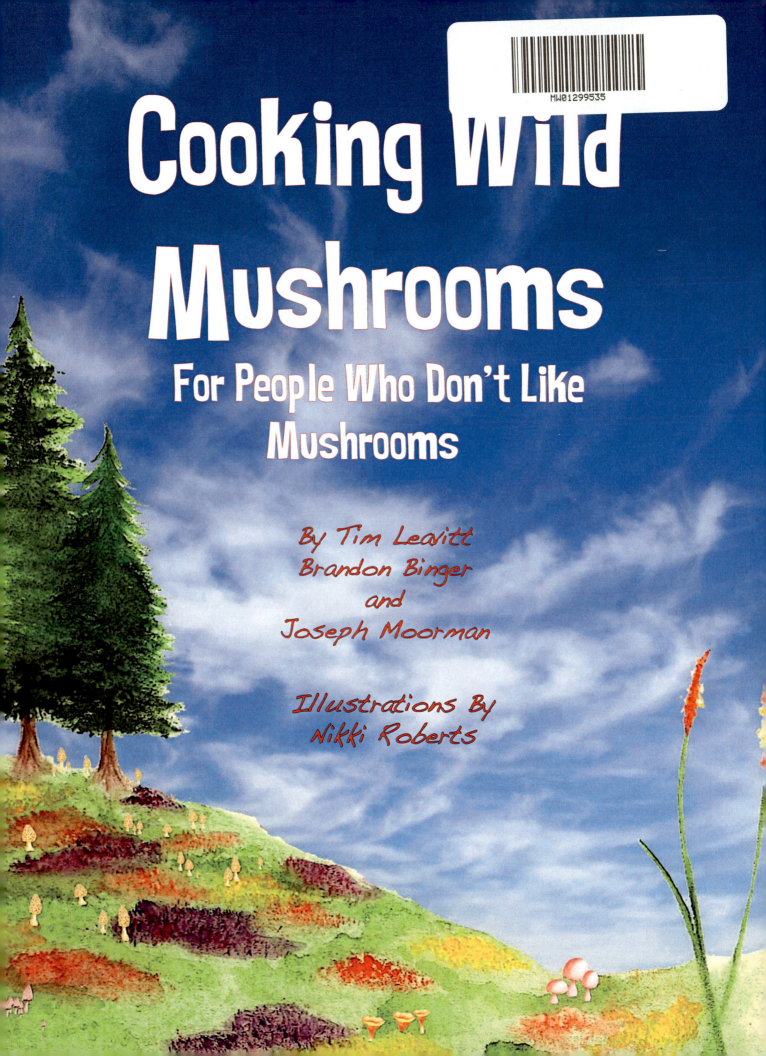

"Cook like an Artist"

Most of the recipes in this book are designed to feed four people, two people that like mushrooms and two that have not yet learned to like mushrooms. The portions are not an exact science. Friends like ours can easily eat six stuffed mushrooms, two Morel burgers, one game hen and half a loaf of bread filled with Morels and brie in one seating.

Cooking mushrooms is as much an art form as a science. In a few recipes, the ingredient volumes have been left out because it is simply impossible to go wrong! Use your common sense and "**cook like an artist**". Based on the ingredients available to you, your unique meal will turn out fine! Enjoy and Bon Appétit!

Table Of Contents

1. Introduction

3. Edith's Mushroom Hunting Tips For Beginners

5. Hydration

7. Basic Wild Mushroom Sauté'

13. The Basic Dried Morel Sauté'

15. Basic Duxelle Recipe

16. Wild Mushroom Compound Butter with Herbs

19. Edith's Mushroom Cooking Oil

20. Pickled Mushrooms And What To Do With Them

23. 10 Year Old Scotch And Pickled Chanterelles

24. Pickled Chanterelle Bruschetta

- 25. Pickled Mushroom Pasta Salad
- 26. Roulade
- 31. Duxelle And Apricot Pork Roulade In Wild Mushroom Jus
- 35. Pork Tenderloin Stuffed With Duxelles
- 37. Edith's Tips For Hunting Oyster Mushrooms
- 39. Tomato Soup And Grilled Cheese with Oyster Mushrooms
- 43. Edith's Tips for Hunting Bear's Tooth
- 45. Chinese Bear Drop Soup
- 47. Edith's Tips For Hunting Morels
- 53. Morel Burgers
- 55. Morel Bread Ball

57. Blackened Black Morel Steaks

63. The Baker's Beef Stew With Wild Mushrooms

65. Edith's Tips For Hunting The Kings

67. The King's Meatballs

69. Wild Rice And Porcini Stuffed Hens With Compound Butter

72. Erica's Porcini stuffed Ravioli

75. Morel Crusted Ravioli

77. Edith's Tips For Hunting Matsutake

81. Grilled Matsutake

82. Brian Pike's Matsutake Fried Egg

83. Matsutake Lettuce Wrap

- 85. Edith's Tips For Hunting Chanterelles
- 89. Gnocci With Orange Chanterelles In A Mushroom Cream Sauce
- 92. Binger's Cream Of Chanterelle Soup
- 93. Hilary's Post Yoga Wild Mushroom "OM"elette
- 95. Chicken Of The Woods
- 97. Basic Chicken Of The Woods Cooking Technique
- 99. The Stuffed Mushroom
- 103. The Northwesterner
- 104. The Classic
- 105. The Greek
- 107. Wild Mushroom Rissoto

This Way!

Introduction

"The mushroom itself is a vessel for delivering the spices and flavorings to your palate. Controlling the texture of the mushrooms and pairing the specific mushroom's subtle flavor with the right balance of spices, foods and wines is the real art of cooking mushrooms."

People say that recipes are not really invented, they are created out of necessity. The same thing could be said about this book. As a mushroom picker, aficionado, the kind of person that has a collection of rare mushroom books on display and a variety of dried mushrooms stashed around his kitchen year round, I am often confused by The People Who Don't Like Mushrooms or T.P.W.D.L.M. This book has been written to convert them, maybe not into full blown mycophiles but at least into People Who Like Some Wild Mushrooms or P.W.L.S.W.M.

As a mycologist, taxonomist, and cultivator of mushrooms I find meeting T.P.W.D.L.M. puzzling. You don't like mushrooms? What does that even mean? It is like telling a botanist that you just don't like fruit. What kind of fruit are we talking about? Bananas? Blueberries? Cooked? Uncooked? Juice? Muffins? Jellies? What are we talking about here? I encounter these people, T.P.W.D.L.M., frighteningly often.

The diversity of species, textures, and flavors available in the mushroom world is similar to the diversity of fruits. Therefore, it is strange to think that because a person dislikes one kind of mushroom, they would dislike them all or even any recipe that includes mushrooms.

The vastness of mushroom varieties is often overlooked. When people hear the word "mushroom", they often think of White Button mushrooms from the grocery store, completely overlooking the diversity of aromas, flavors and textures available in the world of wild mushrooms!

Wild mushrooms, as the name implies, are not cultivated and

therefore are more expensive and harder to aquire than other mushrooms because wild mushrooms are so different and they need to be prepared differently.

I blame the existence of T.P.W.D.L.M. on inexperienced cooks. These cooks are giving the wild mushrooms a bad name. These "cooks" have created T.P.W.D.L.M.

Let's look at an example, a food all cooks are familiar with, the Potato. Any beginner cook knows that you should cook by boiling or baking any potato before frying. Failure to do so will result in a slimy grey mess. Likewise a fried potato chip without some other flavoring would also be considered unpalatable by many. Raw potatoes are seldom served or enjoyed. The problem is the cooking technique, not the potato.

Mushrooms are 90% water and, therefore, it is very easy for an inexperienced cook to make them slimy and gross. Remember when cooking mushrooms, first you need to get the moisture out then put the flavor back into the mushroom. After all, like our potato example, the mushroom itself is a vessel for delivering the spices and flavorings to your palate. Controlling the texture of the mushrooms and pairing the mushroom's subtle flavor with the right balance of spices, foods and wines is the real art of cooking mushrooms.

Fortunately for you, the reader, my colleagues and I have spent years studying these flavor pairings and the subtle in's and out's of wild mushroom cooking. This book is by no means a complete list and a few key species of wild mushrooms have been left out because they do not grow in the author's region. We hope this book will be a good start to converting T.P.W.D.L.M. into People Who Like Some Wild Mushrooms.

Enjoy and Bon Appétit!

Edith's Mushroom Hunting Tips For Beginners

"Get yourself a good knife."

1. Get yourself some taxonomy books! The most important book is "Mushrooms Demystified" by David Arora. Arora has information on just about any mushroom you might encounter in North America. His first hand accounts of encounters with mushrooms makes this abstract subject easier to digest. His book includes a Latin/Greek Dictionary that really helps to demystify the scientific names of your mushrooms.

2. Get yourself a good knife! Different types of hunters use different tools. For mushroom hunters the weapon of choice is a knife, or more particularly knives. A serious picker will have a quiver of knives. You may need a big buck knife or even a machete to cut Chicken Of The Woods off of a tree. A switch blade or Butterfly knife can not only keep your hands free but also scare the mushrooms into just giving themselves up without all of the hiding. Of course, there are also all of the knives you are going to need in your kitchen at home to prepare them, smash them, and cut them into pieces. In the field, the most important knife is a real mushroom picking knife. A mushroom picking knife will have a hooked blade and a brush on the other end. The brush is extremely important for cleaning mushrooms in the woods. If you clean your mushrooms before you put them in your basket you will save yourself a lot of tedious cleaning later. Brushing also helps to knock off some of the mushroom spores and protects future harvests.

3. Don't get lost! Carry a compass and a map. Every season mushroom pickers get lost because they are distracted and looking at the ground. It doesn't take long to become disoriented, so be ready for it! Don't panic! Carry a compass and know how to use it.

4. **Get a basket, bucket or mesh bag!** Mushrooms are designed to be picked. Picking mushrooms will not destroy their mycelium and can actually help them disperse their spores.

The survival of underground mushrooms (truffles) relies completely on the smells they produce. These distinct and strong aromas attract animals like deer and especially squirrels to dig them up and eat them. After eating the underground mushrooms, the animals wander the forest spreading the spores through their feces. Without the help of the mushroom loving animals, these underground organisms would have no way of spreading their spores.

Above ground mushrooms spread their spores by forcibly discharging them into the air. These varieties are not nearly as dependent on animals as their below ground cousins. However, these mushrooms don't mind getting a little help from their friends, and being their friends we like to help them out. While picking mushrooms it is best to keep them in a basket, mesh bag, bucket, or some other unsealed container. This will allow the spores to float away and hopefully procreate while you forage.

"Never trust an "expert"."

5. **Hide.** Whenever possible avoid having people see you picking mushrooms.

6. **Cruise for mushrooms.** Mushrooms are small and usually only show themselves for a few months out of the year. Don't waste a lot of time looking for them, look instead for the places where they live. Mushrooms are very specific as to the ages and variety of trees they hang around (mycorrhiza) and grow on (saprophytes). Mushrooms always follow a pattern. Reading your books will teach you about the behavior of individual species. Once you know the habits of your target species, they will be easier to ambush. When you know where they live and what they eat, you can cruise for them. With experience, you will save a lot of time by not looking in the wrong places. It is a bit overwhelming at first, but you will learn to recognize where mushrooms don't grow and that they only grow in very specific areas.

7. **When trying a new mushroom don't over do it.** Although very uncommon, food allergies do occur in the mushroom world. When trying a new species for the first time only try a small amount.

8. **Never trust an "expert".** Many mushrooms look alike, some can kill you, some can make you wish you were dead! Don't trust somebody just because they say they are an "expert". Double check all your mushrooms with David Arora's book before eating them.

Hydration

The mushrooms discussed in this book are about 90% water and 10% good stuff. This 90% water majority creates one of the biggest problems with cooking and especially with preserving mushrooms.

Mushrooms can be preserved by freezing. However, they must be cooked first. If fresh mushrooms are placed directly into the freezer, the water inside of them will expand and basically crush the mushroom from the inside out. The result will be tragic. If you are going to store mushrooms in the freezer, cook them first, let them cool, and then put them in the freezer.

Dehydration is the most common way of preserving mushrooms. Fresh mushrooms dry at a rate of about ten to one. That is, it takes about ten pounds of fresh mushrooms to make one pound of dry mushrooms. It also means that about one and a half dried ounces equals about one pound of fresh mushrooms and vice versa.

A common kitchen dehydrator works fine for drying your mushrooms. Clean the mushrooms and cut them into as equal sized pieces as possible. Place equal sized pieces of mushrooms together on the same rack in the dehydrator.

Small Morels can be dried whole. Most other mushrooms will need to be dismembered and sliced up into equal pieces. Larger morels should be "butter flied" open. Leave the mushrooms on the dehydrator long enough to get all of the moisture out. After a few hours start sorting through the mushrooms, remove the dry ones and place them into a jar or other sealed container. A single moist mushroom in a sealed jar can ruin your entire stash.

Dried mushrooms will stay good all year. You will find that drying the mushrooms concentrates their flavor and makes cooking with them very easy. There is more flavor in dried mushrooms than fresh, therefore they will have a bigger flavor influence than might be expected from their small volume.

When rehydrating the mushrooms, we encourage you to use more than just water. Think about what you are making and get creative. If you are making orange Chanterelles, add a little orange juice and orange vinegar to your rehydration mix. If you are making a stir fry, rehydrate your mushrooms with a little soy sauce and water. Plan ahead, rehydration is your chance to marinade your mushrooms so why marinade them with just water?

"The mushrooms discussed in this book are about 90% water and 10% good stuff."

Basic Wild Mushroom Sauté

The basic wild mushroom sauté is the cornerstone of mushroom cooking. Master the basic sauté and you will be well on your way to mastering mushroom cooking. Because mushrooms are usually not eaten raw, most recipes start with a basic sauté. The technique will differ slightly depending on the mushrooms and recipes. Remember the common goal which is getting the moisture out first and adding the flavorings and spices second. Good texture will come with practice. This is how we do it and should get you started on the right track.

" Master the basic sauté and you will be well on your way to mastering mushroom cooking."

Step 1: Preheat the pan on medium.

Step 2: Cut up your mushrooms. The style and direction of your cuts will depend on the recipe you are following. Sometimes, you will want to dice them into small pieces, and sometimes you will want to slice them into artistic fans. Whatever your plan, try and keep the mushrooms all pretty much the same size so they will cook evenly.

"*T.P.W.D.L.M. won't like that, and the rest of us won't really appreciate it either.*"

Step 3: Oil the pan. A stainless steel skillet works the best. Use as little oil as possible, just enough to prevent sticking. You want to taste the mushrooms, not the oil. Many beginner mushroom cooks will use too much oil. This not only camouflages the taste of the mushrooms, but can also make your finished product slimy. T.P.W.D.L.M. won't like that, and the rest of us won't really appreciate it either.

As for what kind of oil to use, first we recommend using canola oil. Canola oil has the least flavor of any oil, it is healthy, and it handles high temperatures. You can also use olive oil or butter but these two oils burn at a lower temperature, so we recommend adding a little canola oil to them. The addition of the canola oil to butter or olive oil will make the mushrooms less likely to burn.

Step 4: When the oil is heated, add the mushrooms and sprinkle them with a little salt. The salt speeds up the evaporation rate. Don't overcrowd the mushrooms in the pan, the more surface of the pan that is exposed without mushrooms on it, the easier it will be for the moisture to escape by evaporation. Stir the mushrooms up to evenly distribute the oil and heat. Remember you are trying to get the moisture out, so don't cover them.

"Wait patiently and let them sweat it out for a few minutes."

Step 5: In a few minutes, the mushrooms will realize they are in a pan and they will start sweating. Different species will sweat in different amounts, but they will all sweat. Wait patiently and let them sweat it out for a few minutes. Resist the temptation to stir them. You want the mushrooms to sear slightly. They will release and let you know when they are ready to flip over.

With a little practice, you will learn how to tell when they have had enough. The mushrooms will brown slightly, their external sugars will caramelize and really bring out the flavor. When you think they have had enough, pour off the sweat. If you are making a mushroom sauce pour the sweat back into the sauce. This will not only add moisture, but legitimacy to your mushroom sauce.

Step 6: After the mushrooms are finished sweating, you will need to stir them more frequently. At this time, start adding small amounts of the flavors you are using (lemon, orange, vinegar, garlic, milk, nutmeg, whatever you're using). Stir for about five minutes or until the moisture is gone, the texture is right, and the mushrooms are browning.

Step 7: Turn off the heat. Continue with the rest of your recipe.

Basic Dried Morel Sauté

Experienced Morel cooks will tell you that the only thing better than fresh Morels might be dried Morels. Not only do they have an incredibly long shelf life, but drying Morels concentrates their flavor, cuts down on their strangeness and makes working with them easier. Morels are not to be eaten raw because they will make you sick, so we recommend giving them a quick sauté before beginning on your recipe.

For most recipes, you are going to want to crush the Morels. The best way to do this is with a large knife. If you prefer not to crush the Morels it is fine. The important thing is to rehydrate them by adding the water slowly and in small amounts. Don't just throw them into a bowl of water and strain them out later. Add the water sparingly as it is absorbed by the mushrooms. Be patient and do it right. Don't be afraid to use seasonings and liquids in addition to just water. Rehydration is your chance to marinate your dried mushrooms, so don't be afraid to experiment with what you are using to rehydrate them with. Depending on the recipe, you might want to add a small amount of Worcestershire sauce, milk or even a little nutmeg. Cooking with dried mushrooms eliminates most of the risk of making them slimy and gross. Be confident and try some different techniques.

Photo by Adam Baker

After rehydrating the mushrooms, place a small amount of oil into your pan and preheat to medium. When the pan is warm, add your mushrooms and stir them for about five minutes or until they begin to brown up a little. Remove mushrooms from the pan and continue with your recipe.

Basic Duxelle Recipe

Duxelles, pronounced "duck-SELL," is a French noun for mushroom paste defined as; "a preparation of mushrooms sautéed with onions, shallots, garlic and parsley used to make a stuffing or sauce".

Ingredients

12 oz. Medium Chopped Fresh or Rehydrated Mushrooms of your choice.
3 Cloves Garlic
2 Medium Shallots
1 tbsp. of Butter
1 tbsp. of Canola Oil
2 tbsp. of Italian Flat Leaf Parsley
Salt and Pepper to taste

Step 1: Place the mushrooms, garlic, shallots and parsley in a food processor. Process on pulse until finely chopped.

Step 2: Preheat a large pan on medium heat then add the butter and the canola oil.

Step 3: Cook mushrooms in batches like you would for a mushroom sauté. Sauté for about ten minutes until all moisture has left the mushrooms.

Duxelles can be frozen for a few months or refrigerated for about seven days.

Let your imagination go wild! Duxelles can be used on their own or as stuffings, toppings, in butters, or as garnishes for soups.

Wild Mushroom Compound Butter With Herbs

Compound butters are simply a mix of butter and other ingredients like mushrooms and herbs. The butter is softened by warming to room temperature. The ingredients are added and the butter is remolded and refrigerated. This compound butter is delicious on anything you would normally top with butter. It is also great as a simple sauce for all kinds of meats.

"This is an introduction to butter"

For our example, we are using Morels, but any kind of wild mushroom will produce a unique flavor. Get creative with your butter by adding bacon bits, prosciutto, or a flavored salt. This is an introduction to butter, later on in the book we will show you how to use it with a couple of happy game hens.

Moormansmenu.com

Ingredients

1 Cup of Butter*
1 Handful of Dried Morels
2 Fresh Sage Leaves minced
1 Small Sprig of Rosemary minced, (about 2 tsp.)
1 Green Scallion minced
1/2 Clove of Garlic minced
2 tsp. of Porcini Powder
Pepper to taste
2 Cups of Water
Wax Paper

Step 1: Place 2/3's of the mushrooms in 2 cups of hot water to rehydrate. When rehydrated chop into small pieces and save the broth.

Step 2: Place the butter in a small mixing bowl.

Step 3: Take the final 1/3 of the dried mushrooms and grind them, crush them, or chop them till they are in tiny pieces.

Step 4: Add all of the ingredients into the bowl with the butter. Gently fold them in until the butter is well mixed.

Step 5: Place the butter mixture in the center of a 12" x 12" piece of wax paper, and gently roll it into a log.

Step 6: Refrigerate.

***Please Note:** You can use any type of butter or even vegetable spread. I like European butters and goat butter. Unsalted butters are great as well because you can salt them "just-as-you-like" at the end.

Edith's Mushroom Cooking Oil

Several recipes in this book call for Edith's Mushroom Cooking Oil. Please don't confuse this oil with the oils you are using for your basic sauté. This is not the only dressing that will work, but this is what we use and recommend. Feel free to substitute any Italian Salad Dressing for this ingredient.

Ingredients

- Oregano
- Olive Oil
- Lemon Juice
- Vinegar, Red Wine, Apple, Balsamic
- Ruby Red Grapefruit Juice
- Minced Garlic

Pickled Mushrooms And What To Do With Them

Pickled mushrooms are fun because it's not very often that you see homemade, pickled mushrooms. We recommend Chanterelles, Kings or Oysters for this particular type of pickled mushroom.

Pickled mushrooms are not truly pickled in the traditional sense. In fact, unlike cucumbers, asparagus, or green beans, the mushrooms are actually cooked first before being placed in the oil to preserve them. Giving the mushrooms a "dry sauté" will remove most of the water and improve their texture. Placing the mushrooms in oil will extend their shelf life exponentially. The mushrooms will actually get better with aging, although they will not last forever. With the following recipes, pickled mushrooms won't last long any way.

Even the most committed P.W.D.L.M. can usually be persuaded to chase a pickled mushroom with some 10 year old scotch. In much the same way that tequila and limes accentuate each other, pickled mushrooms and scotch blend perfectly.

Pickled Mushrooms

Ingredients
Chanterelles, Oysters or Kings
Edith's Mushroom Cooking Oil

Step 1: Slice the mushrooms and perform the basic sauté. However, this time use the absolute minimum amount of oil possible, just enough to prevent the mushrooms from sticking to the pan. Basically it's a dry sauté.

Step 2: Place mushrooms in a jar and allow to cool.

Step 3: Cover mushrooms with Edith's Mushroom Cooking Oil. (See page 19)

Step 4: Place the jar on the counter and rotate as often as possible to keep the oil from separating from the other ingredients. Repeat this process for two weeks.

10 Year Old Scotch with Pickled Chanterelles

23.

Pickled Chanterelle Bruschetta

Ingredients
Pickled Chanterelles
Fresh Basil
Tomato
Fresh Mozzarella
Baguette

Pickled Mushroom Pasta Salad

Ingredients
1 Cup Pickled Mushrooms
1 lb. Rainbow Fusilli Pasta
8 oz. Fresh Mozzarella Pearls
1/2 Cup Black Olives
1 Tomato
1 Cup Cashews
Edith's Mushroom Cooking Oil

Step 1: Cook the pasta according to the directions on the box.

Step 2: While the pasta cools dice up the tomato and olives.

Step 3: When the pasta is cool, mix everything in a mixing bowl and add Edith's Mushroom Cooking Oil to taste. Serve at room temp.

Roulade

" Always use high quality meat, this makes a big difference in the overall dish"

Great cooks from around the world have paired the subtle flavors of mushrooms and meat for years. Getting the right balance of mushrooms and meat to the palate at the same time is crucial.

The word "Roulade" is derived from the French word, "rouler" meaning "to roll". Roulades can be made with a number of meats and come in a number of sizes. The important thing is that it is rolled meat filled with tasty ingredients, cooked to perfection, and delivering all of the flavors at exactly the same time. Sizes and shapes aside, a good Roulade looks beautiful and tastes even better.

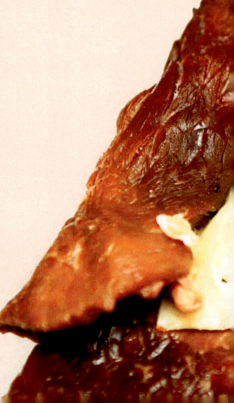

Right, Morels, Bacon, and Jack; far right Matsutake and Crab.

Day 1.

Step 1: Prep the meat. Thin cut round steaks work great for this and are readily available at any meat market. If you don't see what you are looking for right away ask the butcher to cut it for you. An experienced butcher will know exactly what you are looking for.

Tenderize the meat using a meat tenderizing hammer. Place the meat in your marinade and put it in the fridge over night. This mixture will start cooking the meat while it sits overnight.

Basic Marinade
- 6 oz. Mango Juice
- 3 tbsp. Soy Sauce
- 2 tbsp. Worcestershire Sauce
- 2 tbsp. BBQ Sauce
- 1 tbsp. Brown Sugar

Day 2.

Step 1: Take the meat out of the marinade. Discard the marinade and let the meat warm up to room temperature so that it will cook evenly.

Step 2: Get out some toothpicks and soak them in water so they don't burn up later.

Step 3: Get out your ingredients and get them ready. This means cooking the mushrooms, frying bacon and breaking it into pieces, cutting cheese, chopping peppers, or even cleaning crab.

Step 4: Lay the meat out on a cutting board. With artistic considerations arrange the ingredients on top of the meat.

Step 5: Roll the meat up and secure it with toothpicks.

Left, Morels, Bacon, and Jack. Right, Matsutake and Crab.

Step 6: Barbeque roulade to perfection. This is usually accomplished by covering with a piece of foil and rolling the roulade every few minutes over medium heat.

Step 7: Baste with Edith's Steak Sauce and serve. (See page 61)

Duxelle and Apricot Pork Roulade in Wild Mushroom Jus

Pork, apricots, and mushrooms are a magical combination. There are three secrets to this dish. First, brining the pork. Second, to prevent overcooking the pork loin, make sure the stuffing is warm when added. The final secret is cooking the loin slowly on low heat to keep it juicy and tender.

Pork Loin Brine

Ingredients
2-4 lb. Pork Loin
3/4 Cup of Granulated Sugar
3/4 Cup of Salt
10 Garlic Cloves Sliced
2 Bay Leaves
Small Handful of Peppercorns
2 tbsp. of Porcini Powder
(Ground up Dried Boletus edulis optional)

Step 1: In a large pot heat all ingredients until salt and sugar are dissolved. Allow to cool. Add pork loin and refrigerate for 24 hours. This will make the pork extra moist, tender, and full of flavor.

Please Note: Discard the brine, rinse the loin, pat it dry, and allow it to warm up to near room temperature before cooking.

Apricot Duxelles Stuffing

Ingredients
8 oz. of Dried Turkish Apricots processed to fine chop
2 Garlic Cloves minced

Please Note: Using dehydrated mushrooms to make your duxelles will also yield one to two cups of mushroom broth for the Jus.

Follow basic duxelle recipe adding the apricots before sauteing. Add garlic during the last minute or so of cooking. Keep mixture on low heat so it stays warm, but not hot.

Main Recipe

Ingredients
2-4 lb. Brined Pork Loin
12 - 16 oz. of Apricot Duxelles Stuffing
6 oz. of Spinach (optional)
Salt and Pepper

Step 1: Preheat the oven to 225°F. keeping center rack open.

Step 2: Carefully butterfly the pork loin until it is flat and even. Lightly salt and pepper the loin. Then spread the warm stuffing evenly over entire surface and cover with a layer of spinach.

Step 3: Carefully roll the stuffed loin and tie with butcher's twine about every inch.

Step 4: Preheat a large 10 inch to 12 inch cast iron or stainless steel pan to medium high heat.

Moormansmenu.com

Step 5: Pat the loin dry and then brown it until it is nice and crusty.

Step 6: Place the loin in the oven for about 40 minutes at 225°F or until your insta-read thermometer reaches 150°F.

Step 7: Place loin on a plate, lightly tent it and allow it to rest for 15 minutes as you make the Jus.

*Please Note: After removing the meat do not clean the pan the pork was cooking in.

Jus

"Jus" is the French word for Juice. In this particular case, jus refers to mushroom juice served as a dressing for meat.

Ingredients
1 tbsp. Canola Oil (If there is not a tablespoon of rendered fat in the pan.)
1 Large Shallot
1 Medium Garlic Clove
2 Cups Mushroom Broth
1-2 tsp. Brown Sugar (to taste)
2 Bay Leaves
A Sprig of Rosemary or Thyme
1 tsp. of Fresh Lemon Juice

Step 1: Bring the pan the pork was in to medium heat. Add the shallots and cook for 4 minutes scraping the fond (Derived from the French word for "bottom." Fond is the word for the little roasty bits left on the bottom of a pan where something has been cooked and scraped off the pan.) Add the garlic and stir for another minute. Add the broth, sugar, bay leaves, and sprigs, then simmer until liquid is reduced to about one cup.

Step 2: Remove from heat and strain, return to a separate pot over medium low heat. Stir in lemon juice and add salt and pepper to taste.

Step 3: Remove twine from the roast and slice into one inch rounds. Place rounds in the center of a plate and surround with the jus.

Enjoy and Bon Appétit!

Moormansmenu.com

Pork Tenderloin Stuffed with Duxelles
(Alternative recipe)

This is very similar to the Duxelle and Apricot Pork Roulade recipe except we are substituting the pork loin for a pork tenderloin. This is a quick weeknight meal if you already have a stash of duxelles on hand. You do not need to brine the tenderloin and the jus is optional.

Ingredients
1-1/2 lb. Pork Tenderloin
8 oz. of Apricot Duxelles Stuffing-warmed
6 oz. of your favorite Wild Mushrooms for garnish
Salt and Pepper

Step 1: Carefully butterfly the tenderloin, it is very easy to cut all the way through, so be cautious.

Step 2: Stuff, roll, and tie, but be careful not to tie the tenderloin too tight as you may cut into the tender meat.

Step 3: Preheat oven to 300°F.

Step 4: Allow stuffed loin to sit and reach room temperature.

Step 5: Heat a medium heavy bottom saucepan over medium high heat. Add the butter and oil to the pan.

Step 6: Brown the loin making sure all sides get nice and crusty. Then place in 300°F oven for about six to ten minutes until internal temperature reads 150°F.

Step 7: Remove roast to a plate and tent with aluminum foil for ten minutes. During this time, carefully and wearing oven mitts, return the pan to medium high heat. Sauté the mushrooms in the pork drippings, until they are browned, their moisture has been released, and the flavor from the pan has been imparted into the mushrooms.

Step 8: Untie the roast. Slice the roast into one inch rounds, cover it with mushrooms, and serve!

Moormansmenu.com

Edith's Tips For Hunting Oyster Mushrooms

Oyster mushrooms (_Pleurotus ostreatus_ and friends) have a long fruiting period and are usually pretty easy to find. If you find a log out in the woods, you can always just bring it home and water it. It will keep producing mushrooms until the wood is pretty much gone. Oysters are easily cultivated and home growing kits are available from many sources.

Oysters grow on a variety of substrates from straw to coffee grounds and even on old phone books. However, in the wild they prefer hardwoods. In the Pacific Northwest they are most common on dead Alders and Cottonwoods. Further south the same species prefers dead Oaks and Tanoaks. Start looking in the early Fall after the first rains and keep your eyes peeled all the way through Winter.

Tomato Soup And Grilled Cheese With Oyster Mushrooms

After a cold day out picking mushrooms, it's nice to have some warm soup and a sandwich. Oyster mushrooms are a perfect way to turn this normally dull meal into something worth remembering. You can get your soup out of a can or you can follow the recipe here. Pan sauté your Oysters, and this time a few minutes before you finish, add about a tablespoon of lemon and minced garlic. Add these cooked mushrooms to your soup and sandwich.

Soup Ingredients
Oyster Mushrooms
1 Can Diced Tomatoes (about 14.5 oz.)
1/4 Cup Milk
1/2 tsp. Olive Oil
1/2 tbsp. Sugar
2 tbsp. Minced Garlic
2 Leaves Dried Basil
1 tbsp. Lemon Juice

Sandwich Ingredients
Oyster Mushrooms
2 Slices Swiss Cheese
2 Slices Sour Dough Bread
Butter
1 Pinch Black Salt

Step 1: Puree the tomatoes.

Step 2: Put everything except the lemon juice and 1 tablespoon of garlic into a soup pot. Cook it over low heat for at least a half hour.

Step 3: Sauté your mushrooms. Right before they are done add the lemon and garlic. Continue cooking for about two to three more minutes. Add the mushrooms to your soup and prepare your sandwich.

"Oyster mushrooms are a perfect way to turn this normally dull meal into something worth remembering."

43.

Edith's Tips For Hunting Bear's Tooth

For starters Bear's Tooth mushrooms (<u>Hericium abietis</u>) grow on Fir trees. Its close relative, The Lions Main (<u>Hericium erinaceus</u>), grows on Hardwoods.

While trees are alive they produce natural fungicides that prevent saprophytes from growing on them. Therefore, in order to grow mushrooms, the trees must be dead.

Start again in the wetter parts of your state where Fir trees grow. Find an area where trees have been knocked down or broken off (usually caused by wind or avalanches). The Fir trees should be recently downed and dead, although snags and standing dead trees can be just as good. The important thing is that you are not looking for just rotten wood laying on the forest floor. The dead trees should still have bark and still look like trees. When you find trees that match this description check the spots on the tree where it has been broken or the bark has been damaged. That is where you will find the Bear's Tooth fruiting.

The good news is that once you find a spot matching this description that is producing mushrooms, Bear's Tooth will keep coming back for several years. Thus giving you several years to find a new spot.

The mushrooms usually show up a little bit later in the Fall when the forest is good and wet and they stick around for awhile making them pretty easy to harvest. As with Chicken Of The Woods it is not a bad idea to bring along a flat head shovel. The shovel will allow you to harvest mushrooms that might normally be out of reach.

"It is not a bad idea to bring along a flat head shovel".

Chinese Bear Drop Soup

Ingredients
Egg Flower Soup Mix
Bear's Tooth
1 Egg
Sesame Oil

This is one of those simple recipes that is meant to inspire a whole slew of other recipes. Bear's Tooth is the mushroom world's perfect noodle. Get creative and use it in any kind of soup that you might normally add noodles. A few obvious examples might be Chicken Bear's Tooth soup or Minnestrone.

Step 1: Strip the Bear's Tooth down into noodle like strips. Give these noodles the basic sauté. If you like salt, add a little soy sauce towards the end of this process.

Step 2: Mix your soup according to the directions on the package and start heating it in a covered soup pot.

Step 3: Mix the egg up in a bowl and add the mushrooms to the egg.

"Bear's Tooth is the mushroom world's perfect noodle."

Step 4: Bring the soup to a boil. Using a large spoon, stir soup into a mad vortex. Continue stirring while adding the egg and mushrooms. Add a few drops of sesame oil. Stir for two minutes.

Step 5: Serve as an appetizer with your favorite Chinese dish.

Edith's Tips For Hunting Morels

" Morels like most other mushrooms can easily be fooled by the old "I haven't found any for awhile trick!""

Black Morels (<u>Morchella elata</u> and allies) are elusive. Just when mycologists begin to think they understand them, one will do something crazy like show up in somebody's BBQ. For a second we will talk about false Morels and then I will move on to the "When's" and "Where's" of Morel hunting.

False Morels (<u>Verpa spp.</u>), or "Swampies" are not poisonous to everyone, but occasionally make people sick. First of all, they don't grow in the same place as the "true" Morels. They live in almost swampy areas usually around Cottonwoods.

These Verpas are easily distinguished from the true Morel by the attachment of the cap to the stem. False Morels are attached to the stem only at the top in much the

False Morel "<u>Verpa</u>" True Morel "<u>Morchella</u>"

 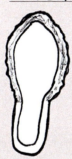

This drawing shows the clear differences between true and false Morels in cross section. Notice the cotton like filaments inside the false Morel and the umbrella like attachment of the cap.

same way as an umbrella attaches to its handle. A true Morel cap attaches straight to the stem at the lower edge. Another easy way to differentiate between true and false Morels is by cutting the stem in half. A false Morel stem will be filled with a cotton like substance. A true Morel will not.

Morels fruit most prolifically in the Spring. When is the Spring? Spring is when there are flowers out and leaves are on the trees.

Morels, especially Black Morels also known as Fire Morels, like disturbance. They will lay almost dormant in the forest until something disturbs them. Then they will shoot up mushrooms and spread their spores.

Sometimes this disturbance is caused by wind storms, floods, or landslides. They can even be disturbed by getting stepped on by an elk or deer, but most often as the name implies, they react to fire. Fortunately, fires are common in the types of forests Morels like, so the mushrooms are relatively common as well. Find areas of burned mixed Fir and Pine forests and you will find Morels.

Another good way to know you are in the right spot is

the presence of plywood signs with the words "Mushroom Buyer" spray painted on them. Migrant workers wandering the forest with buckets are another good clue you are in the right spot.

"When you spot a Morel at a glance never make eye contact and never approach them directly."

fruit. The empty cavities left where a tree's roots have been completely burned out of the ground are also a good spot to look. Also check around wet spots and creeks.

Once you are in the right spot, look around the base of downed trees. A burning tree on the ground will heat the forest floor and cause the mushrooms to

Take your time, move slowly, and attack the

Can you find nine morels in this photo?

Photo courtesy of Adam Baker.

51. mushrooms uphill. When you spot a Morel at a glance, never make eye contact and never approach them directly. Weave your way towards them slowly. Other Morels in the area you might have missed will give themselves up.

Morels, like most other mushrooms, can easily be fooled by the old "I haven't found any for awhile" trick! This trick has been used by mushroom hunters for years. Here is how it works. If you feel like you are in the right spot, but you have not found any mushrooms for awhile, call out to the people you are with "I haven't found anything in awhile!". More often than not, the mushrooms in the area will relax and let their guard down. When they do that, you've got them. Use this trick only as a last resort!

We recommend brushing off all mushrooms in the field. This will help the mushrooms spread their spores and save you a lot of time cleaning at home.

Photo courtesy of Adam Baker

"When they do
got j...

53.

Morel Burgers

T.P.W.D.L.M. are intrigued by Morels maybe because they come up in the Spring, maybe because they are so fun to find, maybe because they are fascinatingly different than your average mushroom.

This is one of the easier recipes in this book. Both easy to prepare and easy to convince T.P.W.D.L.M. to try. Who wouldn't want to try a tasty burger? Start T.P.W.D.L.M. with baby steps while you enjoy your burger topped with sautéd Chanterelles!

Ingredients
Dried Morels
Ground Beef
Worcestershire Sauce

Step 1: Grind up your dried Morels and rehydrate them as you would normally, but this time, add a little Worcestershire to your mix. Sauté them like you would normally.

Step 2: Mix the Morels with your meat and pound out some patties.

Step 3: Barbeque and top with the cheese of your choice.

Step 4: Serve and enjoy hearing T.P.W.D.L.M. tell you that, "they are actually really good" and "they could get used to eating this type of food."

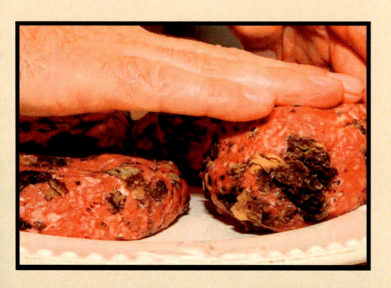

Morel Bread Ball

Ingredients
Dried Morels
Sour Dough Bread Ball
8 oz. Brie
2 tsp. Oregano
2 tbsp. Butter
1 tbsp. Honey
Black Salt
Edith's Mushroom Cooking Oil

Step 1: Preheat the oven to 375°F.

Step 2: Crush the Morels, rehydrate them and give them a quick sauté.

Step 3: Using a sharp knife, cut a circle in the top of the bread ball. Remove it leaving some of the white bread attached to the top. Hollow out the bowl just enough to fit in your wheel of Brie.

Step 4: Place the cheese, mushrooms and oregano into the ball. Add a little mushroom cooking oil and then seal it up.

Step 5: On low heat, in a small pan make a glaze by melting together two tablespoons butter and one tablespoon of honey. Brush this on the bread.

Step 6: Sprinkle with Black Salt.

Step 7: Wrap in foil and bake for 35 minutes.

Step 8: Tear apart and enjoy.

Blackened Black Morel Steaks

Ingredients
Dried Black Morels, lots of them
Steak
20 oz. Root Beer (yes, really)
1 tbsp. Worcestershire Sauce
1/4 Cup Soy Sauce
Oil

Day 1

Step 1: Tenderize and marinade the meat. Use your meat tenderizing hammer to tenderize the meat.

Step 2: Mix together the Root Beer (yes, really) soy sauce and Worcestershire sauce in a mixing bowl. Marinade the steaks overnight. We have all seen what soda pop can do to your teeth so just think about how hard that pop is working to break down and soften up that meat.

Day 2

Step 1: Crush the dried Morels into a fine powder.

Step 2: Preheat the oven to 400°F. This step is optional depending on the thickness of your steak and how you like it cooked. Continue to Step 3 and refer back to this section if needed. After three minutes of searing, your morel crust will be blackened and done cooking. The steak will be pretty rare in the middle at this point. If you like your steak more well done remove it from the heat, cut it in half, flip it, put it on a cookie sheet then into the oven on 400°F for about five minutes.

Step 3: You want the meat to warm up a little before searing. Get it out of the fridge, discard the marinade and put it on a plate about a half hour before you plan on cooking it. Fifteen minutes into this half hour warm up period, press the meat into the crushed mushrooms. During the next fifteen minutes, the crushed Morels will soak up flavoring from the steak.

Step 4: Heat up your cast iron skillet to about medium/high. Let it heat up for about fifteen minutes while you are waiting for the mushrooms to settle into place. If the oil starts to smoke, turn the heat down. Remember, you want the whole pan to be hot not just the oil, so adjust your stove top accordingly.

Step 5: When the skillet is hot and the oil is smoking just a little, drop the steak in and let it sear for three minutes. Don't move it! Let it sit still and sear. After three minutes, flip it over and do the same thing on the other side. Don't move it once it is down. Let the mushrooms cook and the crust adhere to the meat so it does not come off.

Step 6: Remove from the heat, slice thinly, and serve.

Edith's steak sauce is so good her Dad did not want her to publish it here. Once you've tried it you won't go back to eating plain steak again. Here it is: Equal parts soy sauce and lime juice, as much wasabi as you can handle, three to five drips chili oil and sprinkle it with crushed black pepper. Dip your steak in it. You can thank us later.

The Baker's Beef Stew with Wild Mushrooms

Ingredients

1 tbsp. Worcestershire Sauce
6 tbsp. Grapeseed or Olive Oil, add more as needed
3 lbs. Beef Chuck, cut into 1 inch pieces
Kosher Salt and Freshly Ground Pepper
4 Carrots chopped into 1/2 inch rounds
4 Celery stalks chopped into 1/2 inch pieces
1 Onion chopped
6 oz. Can Tomato Paste
2 Cups Hearty Red Wine, such as Shiraz
2 Quarts Beef Stock or Reduced-Sodium Beef Broth
2 Sprigs Thyme
1 1/4 lbs. Russet Potatoes, peeled and cut into 1-inch chunks
1 1/2 oz. Dried Wild Mushrooms (we used dried Morels, Porcinis are also excellent)
4 tbsp. Unsalted Butter
1/4 Cup All-Purpose Flour
Chopped Fresh Parsley, for topping

Step 1: Grab a partner this is more fun with two. Slowly add the wine and one tablespoon Worcestershire Sauce to dried mushrooms to rehydrate them. Then pour yourself a glass of wine.

Step 2: Heat two tablespoons oil in a Dutch oven (we love our cast iron) over medium-high heat. Season the beef with two teaspoons salt and one teaspoon pepper. Add the beef to the pot in batches and cook, turning occasionally and adding more oil as needed until browned all over (about five minutes). Then transfer the meat to a bowl.

Step 3: Add two more tablespoons oil to the pot and reduce the heat to medium. Add the carrots, celery, and onion, and cook occasionally stirring with a wooden spoon and scraping up the fond on the bottom of the pot until the vegetables soften, usually about five minutes. Move the vegetables to one side of the pan and add the tomato paste to the other side. Cook until it darkens around the edge, about two minutes then stir in the vegetables. Finally add one cup wine from the mushrooms and bring to a boil. Pour yourself another glass.

"Grab a partner this is more fun with two."

Step 4: Return the beef and any juices to the pot then add the stock. Bring to a boil and skim any foam off the top. Add the thyme. Reduce the heat to low, cover and let simmer until the beef is tender, about two hours.

Step 5: Using a colander, set over a large bowl, strain the beef and vegetables reserving the cooking broth. Tent the beef mixture with foil. Let the cooking broth stand for five minutes and then skim off the fat on the surface and discard. Return the liquid to the pot, add the potatoes and bring it to a simmer over high heat. Reduce the heat and simmer until the potatoes are just tender, about 20 minutes. Remove the tender potatoes from the liquid.

Step 6: Meanwhile, heat the remaining two tablespoons oil in a large skillet over medium-high heat. Add the mushrooms and cook them by stirring occasionally until they release their juices and brown, usually about ten minutes. If necessary pour off any extra liquid. Season with salt and pepper. Remove from the heat and set aside.

Step 7: Melt the butter in a saucepan over medium-low heat. Whisk in the flour to make a roux, then let it bubble (do not brown) for two minutes. Whisk in two cups of the reserved cooking liquid and the extra wine from the mushrooms. Stir this sauce into the pot with the vegetables and bring to a simmer. Reduce the heat to medium low and simmer, stirring often until thickened, about five minutes.

Step 8: Return the beef to the pot, discard the thyme. Add the mushrooms and simmer until heated through, about five minutes. Sprinkle with salt, pepper, and parsley. Enjoy!

Edith's Tips For Hunting The Kings

(Boletus edulis) (Porcini)

Shortly after the first Fall rains, look for Kings in mature conifer forests located in the wetter parts of your state. If you are in the Rockies, look on the West side of the Continental Divide. If you are in the Pacific Northwest, look on the West side of the Cascade Mountains. If you are on the East Coast, I can't help you I am only six months old.

Make sure your King's have a bulbous stem with a reticulate web type pattern. Although very few Boletes are poisonous, most of them are really not that good to eat. To the untrained eye many of them look similar. People often mistake the King with the Leccinum (pronounced, Lex-eye-num) which has a similar shape, but has black tufts on the stem, not a reticulate pattern. The genus of Suillis is also in the Boletacae family and people do eat them. The name "Suillis" is derived from the word "swine" because they look, feel, and taste like a pigs snout.

Kings get wormy fairly quick, so look for them early in the Fall and look for the little ones. Finding a big King without any worms in it is really uncommon. The big ones are easy to find, but the little ones are usually of better quality.

"Look for the little ones."

66.

The King's Meatballs

Ingredients
1 1/2 Cups cooked King Boletus
1 Granny Smith Apple
1 lb. Pork Sausage
2 tsp. Oregano
Edith's Mushroom Cooking Oil

Step 1: Dice the mushrooms into very small pieces and perform a basic sauté.

Step 2: Cut the apple into very small pieces and grind up the Oregano.

Step 3: Mix every thing together in a mixing bowl. First, make it into one big ball, then divide it up into equal sized balls. The balls will be easier to cook if they are all the same size.

Step 4: Preheat the pan and oil it with a reasonable amount of Edith's Mushroom Cooking Oil.

Step 5: Rotate and roll the meatballs as they cook. You are trying to get them evenly brown on all sides while maintaining their shape.

Step 6: Serve with spaghetti or your favorite Pasta.

Wild Rice And Porcini Stuffed Hens With Compound Butter

Nothing is more enjoyable than picking away at the flavorful pieces of a succulent, small game hen. Stuffing the bird turns it into a complete meal for one. We always recommend making extra rice and butter. Extras make for great leftovers and last minute meals.

Hens
2 Game Hens matching in size
2 tbsp. Compound Butter
1 tbsp. Poultry Seasoning
Salt

Wild Porcini Rice
1 Cup Wild Rice Blend
1 tbsp. Butter or Oil
1-2 Cups Fresh Porcinis or other Wild Mushrooms
1 Shallot (diced)
1 Clove of Garlic (minced)
2 Green Onions (diced)
2 tsp. Fresh Rosemary (minced)
2 Cups of Mushroom Broth or Water

Step 1: Preheat your oven to 375 °F.

Step 2: Remove the giblets from the hens. Allow the hens to rest on the counter as you make the rice. If the center bones of the birds are still cold, the outside will be overdone and the inside of the birds will be undercooked.

Step 3: Cook the rice. First clean it by rinsing in cold water. Next add the oil, butter or bacon fat to a medium sauce pan over medium high heat and stir in the rice coating it with the fat. Then add one teaspoon of salt to the broth and bring it to a boil. When it has reached boiling reduce the heat to low, cover and simmer for 45 minutes. After 45 minutes remove from heat and cover with a towel.

Step 4: Sauté your Porcinis with the shallots. When they are done cooking, stir in the rosemary, garlic, and green onion. Remove the pan from the heat.

Step 5: Get the birds ready. Rub the compound Morel butter under their skin trying not to tear it. In a medium sized bowl mix the mushrooms with the rice and stuff the cavities of the birds. Next rub the remainder of the butter over the birds. Finally, tie the hen's legs together and seal up the cavity.

Step 6: Place the birds either on a roasting rack or heavy bottomed pan and bake for 50 minutes to one hour until the juices of the hen's thigh run clear or your thermometer reads 165°F.

Step 7: If you would like a crispier skin, place the birds breast side up under the broiler for five minutes or less.

Step 8: Let the birds rest for ten minutes. Cut and remove the twine. Add a nice dollop of the Morel butter on top of the bird.

Step 9: Eat.

Moormansmenu.com

Erica's Porcini Stuffed Ravioli

This recipe is very special. It dates back more than 100 years and comes from Erica Leavitt's Italian grandmother. Erica puts a modern spin on it by adding Porcini mushrooms to the ricotta filling making it a delicious dish for mushroom connoisseurs that love Italian food.

You will need a good old fashioned crank style pasta machine to prep the dough for filling.

Please note: Any pasta making machine will do the trick, but the directions below apply to the old fashioned crank style machine.

Ricotta Filling Ingredients
30 oz. Ricotta Cheese
2 Eggs
1 Cup Shredded Parmesan
1 Cup Shredded Mozzarella
2 Cups cooked diced Porcinis
2 tbsp. Dried Parsley
1 tbsp. Minced Garlic
1 Cup Chopped Spinach
1 tsp. Salt
1 tsp. Black Pepper

Dough Ingredients
4 Eggs
1 tbsp. Olive Oil
1/2 Cup Water
1 tsp. Salt
4 Cups Flour

Part One: Make Your Dough.

Step 1: Roll out long sheets of wax paper and sprinkle lightly with flour. You will use these to lay the dough onto after cranking it through the machine.

Step 2: Beat eggs in a large mixing bowl. Add olive oil, water, and salt. Gradually add flour and knead into a nice, round ball. Cover the dough with the mixing bowl and let it sit on the counter for 30 minutes.

Part Two: Make Your Ricotta Filling.

Step 1: Give your Porcinis the basic saute' and then let them cool.

Step 2: Combine all of the remaining ingredients in a large mixing bowl and mix them together thoroughly.

Step 3: Cover and let chill in the fridge while you prepare your dough for filling.

Part Three: Prepare Your Dough For Filling.

Step 1: Take the dough ball and flatten it into a 1-inch thick slab. Using a sharp knife, cut into four equal pieces (see photo at top).

Step 2: Put your old fashioned crank style pasta machine on the largest/widest setting (level seven on most machines). Pinch the bottom edge of each piece of the dough to help it into the machine. Crank each section through the machine and set aside on floured wax paper. Now, adjust the machine to about the middle setting (level five on most machines). Crank the dough through on this setting and then lay it on the wax paper. Your dough is now ready for filling.

> "Put a modern spin on your raviolis by adding Porcini mushrooms to the ricotta filling"

Part Four: Fill Your Dough.

Step 1: Cut the flattened dough into four inch long sections. Put one tablespoon of ricotta & mushroom filling in center of each section (see second photo on left). Fold over the top and gently press on all sides to seal the dough edge (see third photo on left).

Step 2: Use a fork to crimp the ravioli by pressing it into the dough along the edges (see bottom photo on left). This also makes a pretty design around the edges. Depending on how wide your dough came out of the machine, you may have some ricotta filling left over.

Part Five: Boil And Serve.

Step 1: Heat a large pot of water to a rapid boil.

Step 2: When the water is boiling gently toss in about six raviolis at a time so the pot is not crowded. Boil them for about eight to ten minutes. When the raviolis are cooked, they will float up to the top and puff up.

Step 3: Remove from the water and serve with your favorite red sauce!

Morel Crusted Ravioli
(Alternative recipe)

Ingredients
6 Raviolis (see previous recipe for preparation)
1 Cup Crushed Morels
2 Eggs
1/2 tbsp. Milk

Step 1: Preheat the oven to 400°F.

Step 2: Crush about one cup of Morels into a fine powder.

Step 3: In a medium sized bowl beat two eggs and 1/2 tablespoon of milk.

Step 4: Boil the raviolis for five minutes.

Step 5: Dunk the cooked raviolis in the egg mixture and then dip them in the crushed Morels. The Morels won't stick as good as bread crumbs, so you may want to sprinkle them on top as well.

Step 6: Place the raviolis on a wire rack, then on a cooking sheet and bake them for 15 minutes.

Step 7: Remove the raviolis and serve with your favorite red sauce.

Edith's Tips For Hunting Matsutake

The North American Matsutake (<u>Tricholoma magnivelare</u>) are a fairly elusive mushroom. Although they will fruit in the same place year after year, they never seem to show up in the quantity that you want. Matsutake has a reputation in Japan as being an aphrodisiac. For that reason, it occasionally sells for ridiculously high prices. This is the mushroom you hear about selling for 100 dollars each in Japan and often the pickers like my dad carry guns. Putting traditions and speculated medicinal values aside, let's face it, any food with that kind of price tag that is served at a fancy restaurant will act as an aphrodisiac for any would-be suitor.

The Japanese may pay top dollar for these mushrooms, but they don't just slice them up and put them on their pizza. Matsutake are best known

> "This is about the closest thing us mushroom pickers get to what adrenaline junkies call a rush."

and easily identified by their smell, a unique cinnamon aroma provided by the chemical Methyl Cinnamate. The mushrooms are quite fragrant. You will find that a little goes a long way. A few slices will add a special flavor to a whole pot of rice, while

> "Any food with that kind of price tag that is served at a fancy restaurant will act as an aphrodisiac."

at the same time, raising the value astronomically.

The North American Matsutake is most often found in the Pacific Northwest. While it is found on the West side of the Cascade Mountains, it is far more common on the Eastern slopes of the mountain range. The name Matsutake literally translates to Pine (matsu) mushroom (take). Therefore, it seems logical to look for them around Pine trees. In this case, White Pines which commonly grow at higher elevations of the Eastern Cascade forests. Find a middle aged forest with a mix of Douglas Fir and White Pines and you will probably find these mushrooms. I often tell people "look for white mushrooms around White Pines". It seems to be true that both White Chanterelles and Matsutake prefer these types of mature mixed White Pine and Douglas Fir forests.

Enough about the where to look question. An equally important question is when to look. Early Fall, after the first rains is your best bet. Matsutake are most valuable in their immature button phase, so you want to get them early. Preferably, so early that they are still pretty much hidden under the forest duff layer. Look for "mushrumps" which are small humps made in the duff by the mushroom pushing up from below. With a little practice, you will recognize the Matsutake before you dig it out of the duff.

Finding these mushrooms can be tricky because they will grow right along side other mushrooms. One of the Matsutake's common names is the "Pine Spike". This name reflects the shape of the Matsutake's stem which tapers to a point. When you dig one up make sure you get the whole thing.

This tapered stem, the presence of an annulus (ring), cinnamon colored blotches on the cap and the unique smell of methyl cinnamate are the best way to identify Matsutake.

For the experienced mushroom picker, there are few mushrooms that provide the thrill of finding Matsutake in the woods. This is about the closest thing us mushroom pickers get to what adrenaline junkies call a rush!

As Matsutake mature and the cap expands the mushroom decreases in value.

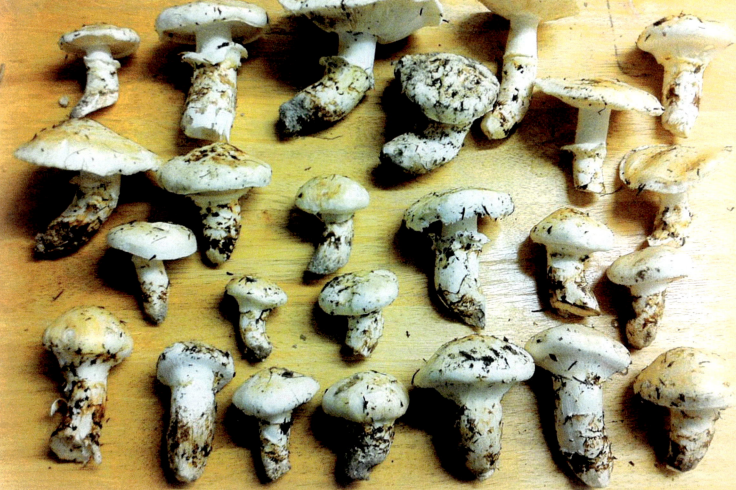

Photo courtesy of Jordan Armstrong

Grilled Matsutake

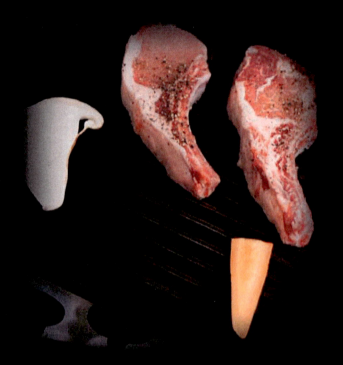

The undeniably unique spicy flavor and aroma of Matsutake makes it a perfect candidate for grilling. Simply cut it into slices and grill it right along side of your favorite meats and veggies. This simple technique is a great way to turn a dull, unmemorable BBQ dinner into something truly delectable. Try pairing your grilled Matsutake with pork chops, carrots and green onions. Then, try it again with steaks, onions and peppers!

Moormansmenu.com

Brian Pike's Matsutake Fried Egg

Ingredients
1 Fresh Matsutake
1 tsp. Butter
1 Egg
Salt and Pepper to taste

Step 1: Heat your skillet on medium heat and swirl the butter into the pan.

Step 2: Slice the Matsutake into 1/8 inch fans and arrange them in a circle in the skillet. Cook for two minutes.

Step 3: Crack your egg and place it in the middle of the mushroom.

Step 4: When the egg starts to brown flip it over.

Step 5: Turn off the heat and let the egg sit in the pan for two minutes.

Step 6: Enjoy!

Matsutake Lettuce Wrap

Day 1.

Ingredients
Matsutake
Beef Brisket
Water Chestnuts
Sugar Snap Peas
Carrots
Lettuce
3 tbsp. Soy Sauce
2 tbsp. Worchestshire
2 tbsp. Horseradish
Chili Oil
Teriyaki Sauce

Step 1: Buy yourself a nice piece of beef brisket.

Step 2: Preheat the oven to 250°F.

Step 3: Put about a 1/4 inch of water in the bottom of a roasting pan. Add the soy sauce, the worcestershire, horseradish, and a few drips of chili oil.

Step 4: Place the meat in the roaster and bake for about five hours or until it pulls apart easily into shreds.

It is a good idea to open the pan and smash the meat with a fork about a half hour before it is finished cooking. Don't worry to much about over doing it, just make sure it shreds easily. When the meat is done let it cool over night in the refrigerator.

Day 2.

Step 1: Slice the Matsutake into fans and give them the basic sauté.

Step 2: In a separate frying pan or wok, preheat about one teaspoon or so of chili oil. Shred the beef into strips and stir fry it along with the water chestnuts, peas, and carrots. Add a little teriyaki sauce toward the end of this process.

Step 3: Clean the lettuce and separate into individual leaves.

Step 4: Assemble the stir fry and the Matsutake on top of the lettuce leaves. Wrap the lettuce around the meat and mushrooms. Serve with Teriyaki dipping sauce.

Edith's Tips For Hunting Chanterelles

There are several kinds of Chanterelles, but for this book, when we use the word Chanterelle in a recipe we are referring to either Yellow (C. cibarius) or White Chanterelles (C. subalbidus). Either of these species can be used interchangeably for any recipe in this book.

Chanterelles can fruit in the same spots for literally decades! So, it is extremely important to protect the secrecy of your spots. If a car drives by or a hiker passes near you while you are picking Chanterelles stop what you are

of the road. You don't want to have to lie to people, so just avoid detection and questions! Otherwise, when you come back next season, the big stash you just harvested might be picked out from under you. Protect future harvests

> "Stop what you are doing, drop your bag, and hide."

doing, drop your bag, and hide. It sounds silly, but even one person at your spot (besides you) is too many. If you are picking at a spot you have to hike into, plan ahead, have a large pack, and hide your mushrooms while hiking out. When you are loading your car, hide your mushrooms. Don't leave buckets of mushrooms sitting out around the parking lot or side

by covering your tracks and always replace any divits you create by digging the mushrooms out of the ground. Leave no trace and no evidence of your activities.

Having said that, it seems obvious that when looking for Chanterelles, you should look for people carrying buckets out in the woods or, better yet, baskets. An old couple walking out of the woods with baskets is an almost sure sign you are in the right spot. Look in the late Summer and into the Fall, but try and get the mushrooms before they freeze. Chanterelles don't freeze well, unless they are cooked first.

Look in mature, second growth forests. Don't look around ferns and don't look in areas where the forest floor is covered with barren duff and few plants. Where there is a diversity of plants, there will also be a diversity of fungus. If you are looking for White Chanterelles, look around White Pines and Firs. Look for Chanterelles around Salal, berries, mosses, vine maples, and stumps. Although they do not grow right out of the stumps, rotten stumps can hold a lot of water and feed fungi diversity.

Gnocci With Orange Chanterelles, Shrimp and Mushroom Cream Sauce

Ingredients
Fresh Chanterelles
8 oz. Brie
15 Cooked Shrimp
Juice from One Lemon
1/4 Stick Butter
Oregano to taste
1/4 Cup Milk
1 crown Broccoli
2 tbsp. Orange Muscat Vinegar
1 lb. Gnocci
1 tbsp. Minced Garlic
1 tbsp. Coconut Oil

Step 1: Put the shrimp in a bowl and drizzle them with lemon juice.

Step 2: Start preparing your cream sauce. Heat a medium sized pan to low. Add the butter, lemon juice, oregano, milk, garlic, and brie. Stir occasionally. Don't let it get too hot.

Step 3: Slice up the mushrooms and begin the basic sauté. Chanterelles are often described as having a "nutty" flavor, so sautéing them in coconut oil will enhance this flavor. As the mushrooms sweat, pour the sweat into the cream sauce. With practice you will learn the timing and you will only have to do this once.

Step 4: Boil some water.

Step 5: When the mushrooms have finished sweating, add the orange Muscat vinegar. At the same time, in the other side of the pan, add your shrimp. Keep the shrimp and the mushrooms on separate sides of the pan. Do not mix them. Stir each one separately, a chop stick works well.

Step 6: Place your broccoli right in the middle of the pan and cover with a lid.

Step 7: Cook and drain your Gnocci. This should only take about two minutes. When the gnocci float, they are done. To keep the gnocci from sticking together, scoop them out using a utensil with holes in it and place them directly into the serving bowl.

Step 8: By this time the broccoli should be bright green, the shrimp should be warmed all the way through and the mushrooms should be perfect. Stir all ingredients together.

Step 9: Top gnocci with the cream sauce, add the mushrooms, broccoli and shrimp. Serve immediately and enjoy!

Binger's Cream Of Chanterelle Mushroom Soup

Ingredients
- 4 tbsp. Butter
- 1 lb. Chanterelles-Coarsely Chopped
- 1 Onion Finely Chopped
- 3 tbsp. Flour
- 3 Cups Chicken Stock
- 1 Cup Heavy Whipping Cream
- 1 tsp. Salt
- 1 tsp. Pepper
- 3 oz. Madeira Wine
- 1/4 Cup Chopped Fresh Parsley

Step 1: Melt butter over medium heat. Add onions and mushrooms, then sauté for about five minutes. If the mushrooms sweat a lot, remove excess water and save for later. There is a lot of good mushroom flavor in the sweat.

Step 2: Add the flour and stir constantly to coat the mushrooms and onions. After one minute, add the chicken broth and bring to a slow boil for five minutes.

Step 3: Remove mixture from heat and blend. This will create a creamy consistency.

Step 4: Put the soup back into the pot on low heat, add the cream, Madeira, salt and pepper. Stir often for ten minutes.

Step 5: Garnish soup with fresh parsley and enjoy!

Hilary's Post Yoga Wild Mushroom "OM"elette

This is a fun way to make a really fluffy omelette. The secret is using butter and whisking the eggs for at least 45 seconds.

Ingredients
4 Slices of Bacon, diced
1 Medium Shallot sliced into thin strands
1 tbsp. Cornstarch
8 oz. Sliced Chanterelles
8 to 10 oz. Chopped Chanterelles or other Wild Mushrooms
1 tsp. Chopped Fresh Thyme or Rosemary
1 Clove Garlic Minced
2 tbsp. Butter
1 Cup of Spinach
Salt And Pepper to Taste
Cilantro to Garnish
4 Eggs Beaten for 45 seconds and Left at Room Temperature

Filling and Garnish

Step 1: In a medium sized frying pan crisp the bacon and drain on a paper towel. Leave the bacon drippings in the pan.

Step 2: Coat the shallot strands in the cornstarch and shake off. Fry in bacon fat until crisp and set aside.

Step 3: In the same pan, sauté the sliced mushrooms until nice and brown, set aside.

Step 4: Sauté the chopped chanterelles. When all liquid has been released add garlic and spinach, cook until wilted. Set the pan aside.

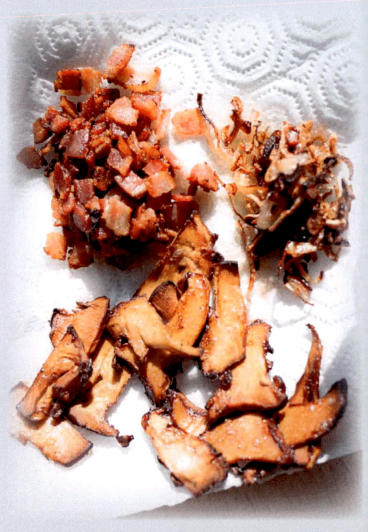

"Om"elette

Step 1: Whisk eggs and 1/2 tsp of salt in a bowl vigorously for 45 seconds.

Step 2: In a large non-stick frying pan, melt one tbsp. of butter.

Step 3: Add the eggs. Using a chopstick lightly stir eggs to fluff.

Step 4: When the "om"elette is almost done cooking, remove it from pan and cover for two to three minutes.

Step 5: Slide the "Om"elette onto a cutting board. Fill with bacon, mushrooms, and 1/2 of the crispy shallots.

Step 6: Roll or fold the omelette, then top with sliced chanterelles and crispy shallots.

Step 7: Garnish with hot sauce if that's your style!

Chicken Of The Woods

Chicken Of The Woods (<u>Polyporus sulphureus</u>) are Polypores and have about 10% less water in them than the other mushrooms listed so far in this book. As a result of this, they are a little tougher than the other mushrooms and require a completely different cooking technique. Good Chicken of the Woods, like good chicken, is cooked slow.

Chicken Of The Woods are bright orange and sometimes the mushroom can cover three feet of the side of a dead tree. Nothing else really looks like them and because there are no deadly poisonous polypores they are pretty safe for beginners. Chicken Of The are so bright and large they can be easily be hunted from the road. Look for them in the Fall on middle aged to old, recently deceased trees or stumps. This mushroom will fruit on different trees from Eucalyptus to Firs and even Oaks. In the Fall look for large dead trees with the bark mostly intact and you should find Chicken Of The Woods.

The freshest specimens are bright orange and very fragrant. As the mushroom becomes older this bright orange color will degenerate to a dull orange and eventually just look pale and gross. These mushrooms can stick around for a long time so look for the freshest part of the cluster that you find. The outer rings of the mushroom towards the edge will provide the softest most delectable meat of the mushroom.

Basic Chicken Of The Woods Cooking Technique

As the name implies, Chicken Of The Woods has a texture similar to chicken. Substitute it in any recipe calling for chicken. We cannot possibly cover all of those, so we will just run you through the basics of cooking Chicken Of The Woods and show you one of our favorite uses of the mushroom: fajitas.

Fresh Chicken Of The Woods is bright orange, fragrant and just a little tough. We recommend cooking it slow. You can cook it in a crock pot, but we recommend a roasting pan.

Step 1: Preheat oven to 250°F.

Step 2: Slice your mushrooms into strips.

Step 3: Oil the bottom of your roasting pan and fill it with about 1/4 inch of water. For our fajita recipe we will add two tablespoons of taco sauce, two tablespoons of vegetable bouillon, two tablespoons of BBQ sauce and one tablespoon honey. Adjust what you add to the water based on whatever recipe you are following. If you are making a BBQ Chicken sandwich, add only BBQ sauce to the water. If you are planning a stir-fry, add some teriyaki. Just don't make the sauce too thick. Be sure to oil the bottom of your pan so it doesn't get ruined. When you are comfortable with your mix, throw in your mushrooms, cover the pan and put it in the oven for at least four hours.

Step 4. After four hours, the mushrooms will be soft and tasty. Sauté them with onions and peppers, then serve with lettuce on warm tortillas.

98.

The Stuffed Mushroom

These recipes go best when prepared with <u>Agaricus campestris</u> also known as the Meadow Mushroom. If you don't have any Meadow Mushrooms, go mushroom picking at the store and pick out some medium sized Button or Crimini mushrooms (<u>Agaricus bisporus</u>). Many stores offer big mushrooms wrapped in plastic and labeled as "stuffers"! Don't believe them, you will get better results from medium sized mushrooms. Mushrooms breath for awhile even after they have been severed from their vegetative bodies, so always keep your mushrooms in a paper bag. When mushrooms suffocate they quickly get slimy and gross.

Step 1: Preheat oven to 375°F.

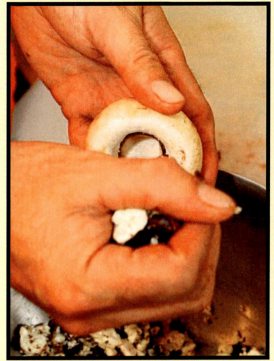 

Step 2: Clean the mushrooms using a brush and luke warm water. Pop the stems out (they should come out fairly easy). Once they are out, you can use a small or sharp bladed spoon to dig out the rest of the stem. This makes more room for stuffing.

Step 3: Using a fork, punch small holes in the cap of the mushroom. These holes should be punched in a concentric pattern and will allow the mushrooms to soak up more flavor.

101.

Step 4: Oil your pan with a liberal amount of Edith's Mushroom Cooking Oil. I usually use a glass pie pan with a metal pan on top but really any bakeware will work. If you don't have a lid, cover the pan with foil.

Step 5: For the first few times stuff the mushrooms with the ingredients listed on the next few pages. Then come up with your own variations. You will find it is pretty easy. People love these mushrooms as an appetizer.

Step 6: Cover pan and bake at 375°F for 20 minutes. You don't have to cover the mushrooms, they will cook faster if not covered which is why most restaurants use this method to prepare stuffed mushrooms. Trust us though, we've done this a lot and the end product will be better if you cover them. After twenty minutes, invite whoever happens to be in the kitchen or nearby to come enjoy the spectacle and the smells revealed as you uncover these beauties. We recommend cooking them for another 20-minutes but each batch will be a little different. So after about 15 minutes turn on the light and watch them cooking. More importantly, watch the oil in the pan, when it turns brown they are done. Don't let the oil turn black.

"Invite whoever happens to be in the kitchen or nearby to come enjoy the spectacle and smells revealed as you uncover these beauties."

The Northwesterner

Ingredients
Cream Cheese
Smoked Salmon
Chanterelles or King Boletus
Bread Crumbs

Step 1: Dice some Chanterelles or Kings into smaller than normal pieces. Give them the basic sauté.

Step 2: Combine all ingredients together in a mixing bowl.

Step 3: Stuff the mushrooms.

Step 4: Dip the tops of the stuffed mushrooms into the bread crumbs, cover and cook.

The Classic

Ingredients
Cream Cheese
Bacon
Dried Morels
Honey

Step 1: Crush some dried Morels into small fragments, rehydrate them, and perform the basic sauté.

Step 2: Fry the bacon, then cut into small pieces.

Step 3: Combine the cream cheese, Morels and bacon together in a mixing bowl.

Step 4: Stuff the mushrooms.

Step 5: Drizzle with honey, cover and bake.

The Greek

Ingredients
Feta
Black olives
Dried Morels
Sun Dried Tomato

Step 1: Crush dried Morels into small fragments. Rehydrate morels and perform basic sauté.

Step 2: Dice the olives and tomatoes into small pieces.

Step 3: Using a mixing bowl, combine all ingredients together.

Step 4: Stuff the mushrooms, cover, and cook.

Wild Mushroom Risotto

In a mushroom risotto, the most important flavor is the mushrooms. First we are going to make a rich mushroom broth. Sauté your favorite wild mushrooms to fold into the rice near the end of the recipe. This adds a nice texture component and prevents mushy mushrooms.

Risotto is an Italian cooking technique that uses a medium grain rice to make a creamy starchy sauce. The most common grain used is Arborio rice. If you prefer, Carnaroli and Vialone grains can be used for a creamier, softer risotto. To achieve the fullest flavor, it is important to use a dry white wine or vermouth early on in the recipe before adding the broth.

"A more rounded dish with hints of all of your favorite mushroom flavors."

Please Note: Mushrooms like King Boletes, Lobster and Morels all have very distinct flavors. Don't limit yourself to just one variety. I like to mix it up with a variety of mushrooms, creating a more rounded dish with hints of all of your favorite mushroom flavors.

Moormansmenu.com

Broth

Ingredients
1 oz. Dried Mushrooms (see note)
1 Bouquet Garni (2 Bay Leaves, 5 Thyme Stalks and a few Sage Leaves tied together with string)
4 Cups of Water
2 Cups of Chicken Broth

Step 1: In a medium pot bring the four cups of water, mushrooms, and bouquet garni to a light boil then simmer for about 15 to 20 minutes until the mushrooms are rehydrated.

Step 2: Strain liquid into another pot. Add the chicken broth and again bring the pot to a simmer. Finally, turn the heat down to low and keep the mix hot.

Step 3: Chop the rehydrated mushrooms and set aside. Discard the Bouquet.

Step 4: Remove the pot from heat and set aside.

Risotto

Ingredients

Broth and Chopped Hydrated Mushrooms (previous page)
Sautéed Wild Mushrooms
2 Cups Arborio Rice (unrinsed)
1 Medium Onion chopped fine
3 Garlic Cloves minced
1 Cup of Dry White Wine
4 tbsp. of Butter (I use Goat Butter)
1 Cup of Grated Parmesan Cheese (optional)
Salt and Pepper
Chopped Parsley

Step 1: Using a four quart saucepan, melt three tbsp. butter over medium heat.

Step 2: Lightly salt the onions and sauté the onions for about ten minutes until soft and clear.

Step 3: Add the Arborio rice stirring frequently for three to four minutes.

Step 4: Add the wine and stir until it is absorbed.

Step 5: Add the rehydrated chopped mushrooms from the broth you made earlier.

Step 6: Add one cup of the hot broth and stir with a flat edged wooden spoon until it is entirely absorbed.

Step 7: Repeat this process adding about a 1/2 a cup of broth each time until it absorbs. Your arm should be burning at this point, but keep scraping the bottom of the pan. It's Okay for your arm to burn, but don't burn the rice.

Step 8: Continue doing this until the rice is cooked and creamy, but still has a little firmness. This should take about 25 to 30 minutes total.

Step 9: Fold in the sautéed mushrooms you made earlier and one tbsp. butter.

Step 10: Stir in the parmesan cheese and chopped parsley.

"It should ooze around the plate, but clump nicely on your fork."

Step 11: Serve.

The texture you want is creamy, but not sticky. It should ooze around the plate, but clump nicely on your fork. The rice should have a little firmness but not be chalky. This is one recipe that takes practice and a strong arm.

About the Authors

Brandon Binger: Photographer. Mushroom Picker. Cook. Brandon has been hiking and collecting mushrooms in the foothills of the Cascade Mountains for much of his life. He helped collect and photograph most of the mushrooms in this book and he makes a mean Chanterelle Cream soup.

Tim and Edith Leavitt: Mycologists. Photographers. Cooks. Tim and Edith have a combined almost 40 years of mushroom picking experience in the West. Tim studied taxonamy with David Hosford at Central Washington University and studied cultivation with Paul Stamets. Tim has worked as a mushroom cultivator, mushroom landscaper and a mycologist involved with the creation of Enviromental Impact Statements for the U.S.F.S. He has lectured 4th grade classes, universitiy classes and at P.SM.S meetings. Tim and Edith have more secret mushrooms spots than most pickers have spots.

Joseph Moorman: Cook. Photographer. South African raised Joe Moorman has a passion for cooking and photography, he loves the outdoors and mushroom hunting. While working on this book, we sent him down weekly shipments of our findings. These mushrooms were then prepared to artistic culinary perfection and the recipes were submitted for this book. Follow more of Joe's cooking on his blog, Moormansmenu.com.

Thanks for joining us!
Bon Appétit!

Special thanks to: My Mom Doris, Erica, Hilary, Ian, Jordan, Clarke, "Crabby" Matt Cupp, Anna Yost, Brian Pike, Adam, and Andrea Baker.

Made in the USA
San Bernardino, CA
03 September 2015